MANUFACTURED IN MALAYSIA
January 2010
10 9 8 7 6 5 4 3 2 1

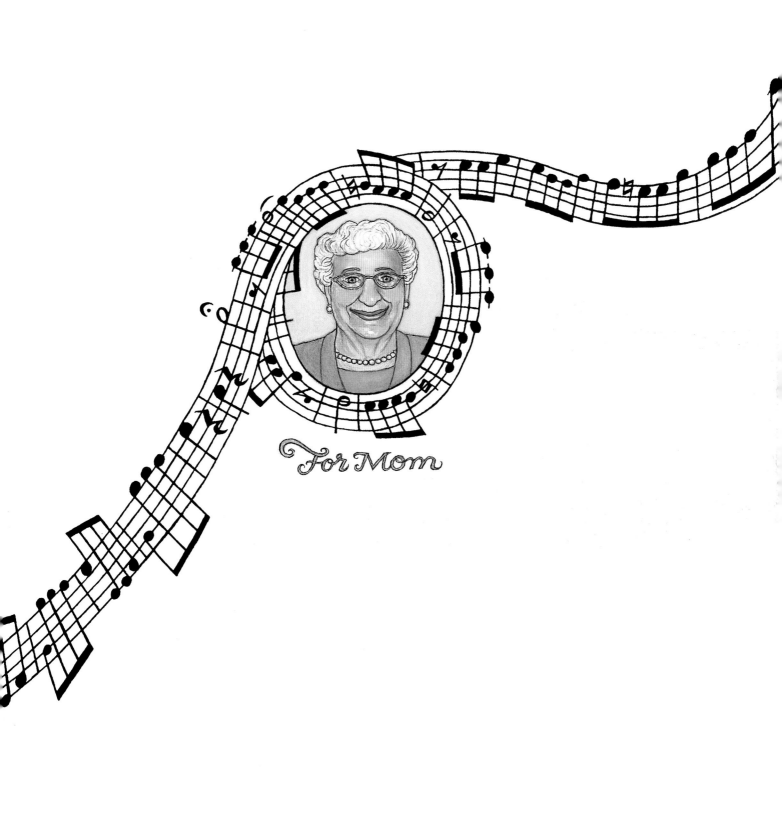

For Mom

THE DAY I TURNED EIGHT, IN 1955, MY PARENTS GAVE ME A REALLY COOL BIRTHDAY PRESENT.

IT MIGHT NOT SEEM SO GREAT TODAY BECAUSE THE WORLD HAS CHANGED SO MUCH.

BACK THEN, LOTS OF THINGS WE NOW TAKE FOR GRANTED DID NOT EVEN EXIST. THINGS LIKE PERSONAL COMPUTERS, CELL PHONES, VIDEO GAMES, VIDEO CAMERAS, IPODS AND CD'S.

TELEVISION WAS BLACK-AND-WHITE AND MOST HOMES HAD ONLY ONE. OR NONE AT ALL.

IN OUR HOUSE, BESIDES OUR TV, WE HAD ONE BIG RADIO IN THE LIVING ROOM THAT WAS SHARED BY ALL THREE OF US.

SOME OF THE BOYS IN MY CLASS STARTED COMBING THE PARTS OUT OF THEIR HAIR AND ASKING ME FOR STYLING TIPS.

HOW DO YOU GET IT TO PUSH UP LIKE THAT?

MINE ALWAYS GOES FLAT.

MINE ALWAYS COMES OUT CROOKED.

ONE DAY MRS. FABER SAID I COULD RESTYLE THE HAIR OF ANY BOY IN OUR CLASS WHO WANTED TO TRY IT OUT. MOST OF THEM DID AND, ONE BY ONE, I GAVE THEM EACH AN ELVIS POMPADOUR.

MY ELVIS REPUTATION SPREAD BEYOND OUR CLASS. ONE DAY, BERT KELLY, A *REALLY COOL* FIFTH GRADER AND ELVIS FAN, ASKED TO SEE MY SCHOOL PHOTO.

MAN, YOU REALLY *DO* LOOK LIKE HIM!

SOON WE BECAME GOOD FRIENDS, SHARING OUR INTEREST IN ELVIS.

WOW! I'VE NEVER *HEARD* THESE RECORDS!

YEAH, THAT'S SOME OF HIS EARLY STUFF.

THEN CAME THE NIGHT OF THE BIG EVENT. AS MY FATHER PULLED INTO THE COMMUNITY CENTER PARKING LOT AND I SAW ALL THE CARS AND PEOPLE, I BEGAN FEELING SOMETHING ELSE: NERVOUS!!

INSIDE, THE AUDITORIUM WAS REALLY CROWDED. THE WHOLE CUB SCOUT PACK WAS THERE, ALL THE SCOUTS AND PARENTS, SOME BROTHERS AND SISTERS, AND EVEN A FEW GRANDPARENTS.

THE CURTAIN OPENED. I SAW THE CROWD. ALL EYES ON ME! COULD THEY SEE HOW NERVOUS I WAS? COULD THEY TELL I WAS SHAKING?

THE MUSIC BEGAN — LOUD AND CLEAR — AND ANOTHER FEELING SHOT THROUGH ME. THAT ELVIS FEELING! IT GOT ME MOVING AND SINGING.

SUDDENLY, I WASN'T SO NERVOUS. MY BODY WAS STILL SHAKING, BUT THAT ONLY MADE ME BETTER. SHAKING WAS WHAT ELVIS DID! AND, *BOY*, WAS I SHAKING! MOVING LIKE I'D NEVER MOVED BEFORE, DOING EVERY MOVE I'D PRACTICED ALL THOSE HOURS IN MY ROOM AND MAKING UP NEW ONES RIGHT THERE ON THE STAGE!

I FELT THE CROWD REACTING, TOTALLY WITH ME. SOME LOOKED SURPRISED AT HOW I WAS MOVING. I WAS SURPRISING MYSELF. THIS WAS LOTS MORE FUN THAN DOING ELVIS ALONE IN MY ROOM.

NEAR THE END OF THE SECOND SONG, I SWUNG MY ARM IN A CIRCLE, LEAPED IN THE AIR AND CAME DOWN ON ONE KNEE ON THE LAST NOTE.

THE CROWD WENT WILD, APPLAUDING, CHEERING, WHISTLING, SCREAMING, GIVING ME A STANDING OVATION.

These are some photos of Elvis-related moments from my life:

My third-grade school photo, the year I first discovered Elvis.

My fourth-grade school photo, which Mrs. Faber said looked like Elvis.

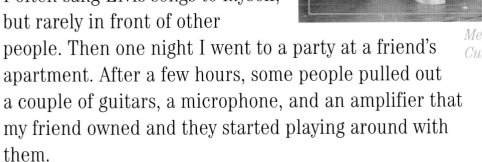

Me doing my Elvis at the Cub Scout dinner.

As I grew into adulthood in the years after the Cub Scout dinner, I often sang Elvis songs to myself, but rarely in front of other people. Then one night I went to a party at a friend's apartment. After a few hours, some people pulled out a couple of guitars, a microphone, and an amplifier that my friend owned and they started playing around with them.

I asked if they knew any Elvis songs. They did. So I took the mike and started singing and wiggling. Everyone loved it.

Then my friend got the idea that we should form a band and put on an Elvis show. Which we did. It was a big hit. Over the next several years, we put on a bunch of Elvis shows at private parties in various theaters, nightclubs, art schools, and lofts around Manhattan.

For many years, I was a political cartoonist for the *Washington Post.* In those days, the *Post* held a special dinner once a year for a small group of political cartoonists, journalists and politicians. At the end of each of those dinners, I would be called on to do my Elvis, a cappella.

In 1993, someone arranged for our group of cartoonists to have a one-hour visit with President Clinton and Vice President Gore in the Oval Office of the White House. The Vice President had once before seen me do my Elvis. He also knew that the President was an Elvis fan. After a while, he spoke up and said: "In his lifetime, Elvis only visited the White House once, but he's here among us today."

That was my cue to do my Elvis for the President. I took off my tie and jacket, turned up my collar, and did my rendition of "All Shook Up."

The President liked it so much he sent an aide upstairs to bring down an Elvis necktie he had in his closet, which he signed and gave to me.

I still have it (of course), safely tucked away, a

valued memento and one of the many cool things that my love of Elvis has brought into my life.

These photos show the transition from my real self into Elvis.